The Psychology of Bagels

Carrie KC West

The Psychology of Bagels

ISBN-10: 0988382318
ISBN-13: 9780988382312

DEDICATION

For Simon, my favorite bagel.

The Psychology of Bagels

CONTENTS

ACKNOWLEDGMENTS

To the Great and Wonderful Murray for his inspiration and passion for all things bagel; to the Band of Bagels for their commitment to what is now known as "The Book" and to everyone that has ever enjoyed a bagel; past, present and of course the future and made this possible. I want to especially thank Thelma who has believed in me since the beginning.

1 INTRODUCTION

I love bagels.

When I think about those three little words I can't help but wonder, "What's not to love?" Bagels are tasty, come in a variety of flavors to please your every whim and can be (perhaps should be) enjoyed throughout the day. For

breakfast, I love a plain bagel slathered in cream cheese that is melting from the light toasting. At brunch, I'll add tomato and just a paper-thin slice of lox. If I'm feeling particularly adventurous, and if they have them, I'll switch to a sun-dried tomato bagel. Delicious.

At lunch there are even more options. I can have a bagel dog, pizza bagel or a bagel sandwich with anything from tuna to turkey or roast beef. I've often thought that the bagel industry could use a new slogan. How about: "Bagels. Not just for breakfast anymore." Catchy, yes?

So how did I come to be so enamored with bagels that I took the time and energy to write this book?

One day, while working for a client in Los Angeles, I decided to entice people to an early morning meeting by promising bagels. I brought in a bag full of fresh right-out-of-the-oven bagels, from a local shop that I found to be among the best bagels in the area. The drive was at best a challenge as the aroma of freshly baked still warm bagels filled my car. My mouth watered uncontrollably. It took every ounce of will power not to grab one and bite into the warm dough as I drove.

When I arrived at the office, I quickly went into the conference room and ripped the bag so that the bagels would fall randomly on the credenza along the wall. I opened the container of whipped cream cheese. This particular bagel shop provided a great variety of bagels and I was certain to have something for everyone. Imagine my complete and total surprise when six of the ten people wanted cinnamon raisin (there were two) and two others wanted blueberry (there were exactly zero). Luckily one man wanted a poppy seed. That was it. The sesame, everything, garlic and onion remained. In fact, during the day when people came by to grab a bite as they do when there is food around, they took everything but the garlic and onion. I was shocked. The next time I tried the bagel experiment, I brought mostly cinnamon raisin and threw in a couple other sweet types – cinnamon sugar, cranberry, blueberry and chocolate chip. The bunch of them was gone in thirty minutes.

That led me to wonder. Is there a pattern to the bagels

we favored? Was there some underlying pattern in social behaviors that were similar among people that liked the same kind of bagels? Working with a psychologist friend, I developed a quiz that checked for qualities that we all have in common in one form or another. I then asked fifty people to complete the quiz and found that there are some characteristics in common that may impact your choice of bagel. Is it a perfect science? No, but it is a fun way to learn about ourselves. It was also a great excuse to research this food that has been a part of our culture for decades and probably will be so long after I've gone to that big bagel shop in the sky.

Do me a favor and take the quiz that you'll find in the appendix or online at www.thepsychologyofbagels.com. See where you fit in with your answers. And while you're at it send me your favorite bagel story. If it's a good one, I'll add it to the book and website. That also goes for any ideas on types of bagels that you eat that aren't mentioned and types of schmears that you enjoy. Be sure to include your first name and the city where you live.

2 BAGELS: A BRIEF HISTORY
(IN CASE YOU'VE EVER WONDERED OR CARED HOW BAGELS BECAME A PART OF OUR LIVES)

The research on bagels while consistent as to dates and times and events often times, I found, written without mentioning that most of the immigrants and founding groups were Jewish. To be sure, there is some mention of the Jewish community's undeniable contributions to bagels and their value in our current culture. In our unending need to be politically correct and never offend, I am making my first and hopefully only disclaimer of this book. I am stating clearly and for the record that bagels are a Jewish food, introduced to North America by Jewish immigrants and created by Polish Jews in the early 17th Century. And I can't help but wonder if the omission was simply because we all assume and agree on that fact.

Now, on to the history.

Most agree that bagels had their origins in Poland in the

early 1600's. It's interesting how the name "bagel" rose to prominence. During the 1610's it was common for a soft, crusty, warm bread, that was chewy and delicious, to be given to women and mid-wives as a gift during childbirth. The bread was known as a "bajgiel" (In Cracow Poland it was called "beygl") and both refer to a type of bread that is "toroidal' (that means round) in shape. Today, both words are translated into the commonly known "bagel". Others sources claim that the first bagel rolled into the world many decades later when in 1683 a Viennese baker paid tribute to King Jan Sobieski of Poland. The King had just saved Austria from a Turkish invasion that would have annihilated the country. Since the king was a great horseman, one inventive baker came up with the idea to make a bread treat in the form of a stirrup (or 'beugal') to honor the king. Some sources also list the German word for 'ring' ('beigel') and 'bracelet' ('bugel') as other possible origins for the name.

It seems we were destined to have bagels in our modern day culture.

Bajgiels/beygls/beugals made their way to North America along with the influx of immigrants from Eastern Europe looking for the promise of a better life in the late 19th century. These brave people may have left their homeland but they brought with them their passions for food and their way of life. One group of immigrants landed in the United States; another group in Canada, primarily in Toronto with groups making their way to Montreal, just like a great influx of immigrants to New York also made their way to Philadelphia for this area, too, became a center of influence for the future of bagels. Interestingly, there were many similarities between the regions where the immigrants chose to make their new home: multitudes of people from around the world arrived regularly, a largely accepting notion of the new cultures brought together in the New

World and a similar arrangement of soon to be growing metropolises, with large areas of space where markets and shops could be arose.

At first there were a great many similarities. In all locations, the bagels were easy to make and sell. Imagine being able to load up a fresh batch of hot doughnut-shaped bagels on long wooden pegs to show your wares at the hugely popular markets of the day. Many women often took advantage of the torus shape to string the bagels along and carry them wrapped around their bodies. The tantalizing aroma of fresh baked bagels filled the air. Workers stopped, grabbed a hot crusty delight off one of the wooden rods or strings tossed the baker a penny or two and went on his way. Delicious. Though separated by hundreds of miles both areas continued to prepare bagels in the same way, maintaining the integrity of the process.

Bagels are unique from any other breads in that the once prepped; the dough is first boiled before they are baked. It is the boiling that brings the chewy dough and crusty crust that defines a bagel. As for flavors, poppy seed and sesame were most popular along with the plain variety. On very rare occasions, bakers added tart and tangy onions and garlic. The egg bagel was common, too because at that time, eggs were added to the recipes.

And here is where we have a divergence in culture and styles when events of the new century brought a great divide between the two regions.

During World War I, there were a couple of shortages in the United States that changed the style of bagels in the country. The rationing of sugar and eggs forced bagel bakers into a new way of thinking. Faced with the possibility of ending their bagel production, these brave immigrants, travelers from thousands of miles for a better life, determined to find an answer. And so the egg-less bagel – and first of what would become the hugely popular New York Style or Water Bagel – was created. The creative bakers also determined that they could still maintain a good chewy bagel by using only enough sugar for the yeast and completely eliminating the use of any sweeteners in the water used to boil the dough.

Even now, the differences in ingredients between the Montreal and New York bagels are mostly around the inclusion of an egg and sugar in the Montreal-style recipe. That and the use of some type of sugar in the boiling water, but we'll get to that and more in a moment.

The popularity of bagels in the eastern region of the United States grew so strongly that the International Bakers Union was formed in 1907. At the time, the union brought together 300 artisans of the craft and prevented anyone but the sons of members to learn the secrets and safeguard the process of making bagels by hand. Without this forethought, it is impossible to say how the bagel we enjoy today would have been altered to meet other personal agendas. Still, when the difficult question of how to automate the process of making bagels was finally answered in the early 1960's the International Bakers Union was disbanded. And here's an interesting note. At the time of the union's demise, the total number of union members rose to a mere 350 people, manufacturing 250,000 bagels a day. By hand.

With the advent of a mechanized bagel manufacturing process, production rose to millions of bagels a day bringing a new surge in popularity to bagels and spreading bagel aficionados further west. It also brought with it frozen and pre-packaged bagels that are sold in every market around the country.

It wasn't until the 20th century that bagel varieties grew to include cinnamon, raisins, salt and whole wheat with the more gourmet types of pesto, sundried tomato, blueberry, pumpkin and apple to arrive later that century. And the popular egg bagels were once again added to the growing list.

Even though many people enjoyed a variety of bagels, the emergence of spreading bagels with cream cheese schmears also arrived in the 20th century, with a variety of schmears – fruit, savory and spicy flavored – joining the mix around the time the popular bagel eateries appeared. The practice of eating lox with bagels came with the arrival of immigrants from Scandinavia in the later 19th/early 20th century. The Scandinavians brought their love of salmon, particularly thin sliced and smoked. The thin sliced treat combined to form a perfect meal when eaten with bagels.

Although many would argue, myself included, that the best bagels are handmade and fresh out of the oven, nothing compares to the ease of eating and enjoying a just-toasted bagel covered in cream cheese or your favorite spread.

Montreal vs. New York

As mentioned earlier, up until World War I, all bagels contained eggs and sugar was added to the boiling water. They were also baked in wood burning ovens, which was the typical oven of the day. It wasn't until the early 20th Century that gas ovens found their way into the mainstream usage and at that time, most bakers in Montreal held firm with baking in wood burning ovens, a practice that continues today.

The distinction between Montreal and New York bagel goes beyond the inclusion of eggs and sugar. In the preparation process, Montreal bagels are boiled in water that contains sugar, honey or malt, adding to the sweetness of the dough and somewhat of a sheen on the finished product. Then the Montreal bagels are baked in wood burning ovens. The result is a sweeter, crunchier more bread-like roll rather than the puffier, often described as 'bloated' or 'pillowy" looking New York style bagel. Another distinction is that Montreal has only three types: black seed (poppy), white seed (sesame) or plain. The final difference and I'm not sure why this is important but it's come up several times now when talking to people, is in the shaping of the bagel. New York-style bagels are shaped by forming a ball of dough and placing a finger or some kitchen device in the center to 'poke' a hole in it. Montreal-style bagels are formed by rolling a long strip of dough and then joining the ends to form a ring. The resulting shapes are still similar and yet after baking and tasting there are differences. In truth, all of the differences in preparation from the ingredients, to the rolling, to the baking in wood burning ovens do create a different bagel.

No matter what, it is ultimately a matter of taste. Many people argue for the Montreal-style and we will always have our die hard New York-style followers. The choice is yours.

3 EATING BAGELS: NOT JUST FOR BREAKFAST ANYMORE

The latest statistics on bagels showed that in a one year period ending May 2011, American spent over $1 billion – yes that is BILLION – on bagels. Is it any wonder that with that kind of money at play, we will come up with new and improved ways to take a bite out of the bagel market?

Bagels are mostly thought of as a breakfast food. More bagels are consumed during the morning – either at work or at home – than any other time of day. It's easy to just pop one in the toaster, cover it with cream cheese or butter and enjoy with coffee or juice. The practice of bringing a dozen or so to the office as a treat to employees contributes to the perception and fact that mornings are made for bagels. Plus, with the increase of gourmet coffee consumption and the smart business minds that run our country, you can now purchase a bagel with cream cheese or butter to go with your latte or mocha.

On weekends, we have some flexibility in our eating

schedules. Brunch is the second most popular time to consume bagels and not surprisingly, bagel lovers are more likely to add lox at brunch than at any other time of day. That makes sense when you think about it. Brunch is that in-between meal when it is perfectly fine to have bacon and eggs or a salad and sandwich. An open face bagel with cream cheese and lox gives you the best of both meals: a sandwich with a typical breakfast food.

One of the more fascinating things about bagels is that they are adaptable. We talked about how this traditionally Jewish food is now popular with any person of any spiritual interest, ethnicity and heritage. Seriously. While bagels are primarily an American pastime, they can be found all over the world and are enjoyed by people from all countries. And if anyone is reading this from somewhere other than the United States, please send a shout out and let me know about your bagel experiences. It really is a fascinating story.

Secondly, bagels have changed according to our changing food tastes. And while I will probably never eat a chocolate chip bagel, I can certainly, as a chocoholic, appreciate the interest in them. Same with the black Russian, banana raisin and some of the other sweeter varieties – I am just not someone who likes sweet bagels. On the other hand, I love love love spinach, pesto and sun-dried tomato bagels and would carry them with me in a bag and eat them all day if I wasn't so afraid of gaining 4000 pounds. The point is, bagel varieties have grown to meet the ever expanding taste buds of the people who enjoy them.

And with the new varieties comes the expanded opportunities to eat them. Noah's Bagels makes my favorite bagel dog. They use all beef hot dogs and just the right dough, still boiled before it is baked, with the hot dog inside. In my, of course humble opinion, they are delicious. The juices from the hot dog melt into the dough and the chewy texture of the bagel just works. Some bagel shops even add the fixings to the dough after boiling giving you the choice of an everything, garlic, onion, or poppy seed bagel dog.

Next up on the list: sandwiches. I'm going to go out on a limb and say that every bagel shop in the entire world offers a plethora of sandwiches using any variety of bagel they sell. The unique chewy flavor of the bagel, along with tuna, turkey, roast beef or ham add a new dimension to the sandwich experience and certainly give you a break from your whole wheat bread slices. Plus, you can eat them open faced, using only half the bagel thus saving precious calories, or you can have two sandwiches meaning you now have to spend an extra half hour at the gym. Either way, the choice is yours.

And where would we be without the pizza bagel? While rising in popularity at your local bagel shop, they are also quite easy to prepare at home. And they make a wonderful addition, and some would argue healthier option, to the variety of snack food we eat.

Here's what you do:

Take your favorite bagel, slice it in half (watch the fingers, no BRI's please) and cover each half with tomato sauce. Grab a hand full or two of shredded mozzarella, and spread it on the bagel halves. Now you add pepperoni on one side and veggies on the other for even more variety or just add your favorite pizza toppings to both. Bake the bagel pizza at 350_b0 for ten minutes or until the cheese is melted and slightly bubbling. Let it cool and enjoy. Cooling is important. The hot cheese and toppings will burn you faster than you can imagine and burning your lips or the roof of your mouth is not fun.

The Phenomenon Grows

In 2011 Dunkin Donuts well known for its great regular coffee and donuts, added to its bagel menu by introducing the Bagel Twist. The bagel twist uses the same recipe and is boiled before baking. The difference is in the shape, which in essence, and as the name implies, means the dough is twisted into five inch strips, making it a bagel without a hole, and quite similar in appearance to a cruller. Some of the sweeter varieties have a line of icing drizzled across the top. And I wonder; Is Double D's trying to create a donut bagel? Isn't part of the definition of it being a bagel is the shape? Just saying...

Another new style of bagel was born in 2011: the bagel thin. They are billed as a regular bagel only thinner. These thinner bagels were first introduced by Thomas and can now be found in bagel shops everywhere. While the thinner bagels have fewer calories there is something missing when you take away the pillowy chewy taste of a regular bagel. I'll pass.

And it seems that everyone is getting in the bagel game. Snack food companies have started packaging and selling bagel chips. To be fair, some bagel shops thinly slice their day-old (let's face it – getting stale) bagels and sell them to their customers. They are easy to eat and take advantage of the flavorful varieties of the bagel they are made from. They are great with dips, soups, salads or right out of the bag.

Bagels have grown as our tastes have changed. So where will we go from here? That's hard to say. But I will bet you a dozen bagels that someone or something will create a new food using bagels in the next five years. Count on it.

For me, I am content with regular bagel and cream cheese.

4 FIRST SCHLOP ON THE SCHMEAR

Let's talk about schmears.

"Schmear" has a few different spellings; from schmear to shmear to shmeer and schmeer it's enough to ruin any spell check program. Several online dictionaries agree that a schmear refers to a group of things that go together as in "they got the whole schmear". These same dictionaries also agree that a 'schmear' refers to the cream cheese found on bagels. Although schmears has become a catchall word referring to any kind of spread that go on bagels, most consider cream cheese to be THE schmear when we talk about schmears.

From Dictionary.com, the definition of a "schmear" is: "a dab, as of cream cheese, spread on a roll, bagel, or the like." One question. How big is a 'dab'? In my mind it's about a quarter of a cup. On each side of the bagel. Just saying. The 1999 Encarta World English Dictionary, defines a "schmear" as "something such as cream cheese spread on a roll or bagel," while the Internet's Urban Dictionary in 2000 defined "schmear" as "a large spreaded 'schlop' of cream cheese usually schlepped all over a bagel." Today, the Urban Dictionary merely defines 'schmear' as "NYC Deli slang for the act coating a bagel with a small amount of cream cheese, or; a small amount of any condiment applied to a food item." My have times changed.

How the word "schmear" came to be associated with cream cheese is a little open to interpretation.

Urban legend says "schmear" a word Yiddish in origin, was first associated with bagels when someone, probably an American Jew, ordered a bagel and cream cheese by saying: "Gimme the whole schmear, will ya?" meaning, a bagel , toasted with cream cheese. Probably many someone(s) were ordering the same way because over time, the concept of a schmear spread. And now it is mostly, if not exclusively associated with bagels. Have you ever seen someone order toast with a schmear? Me neither. And while we're at it, do you put cream cheese on a piece of rye toast? Rye bagel, of course. But not on rye bread. In all my days of eating English muffins, toast and other high-carb breakfast breads, the only one that makes sense to have schmeared with cream cheese is bagels. I've tried them all and it just seems that bagels and cream cheese work in ways uniquely its own.

In any case, "schmears" came to be seen mostly as something on a bagel. I say 'something' because if you go to any bagel store anywhere, the variety and types of schmears has grown well beyond a traditional dollop of cream cheese.

But let's not get ahead of ourselves. In order to understand how a schmear turned into cream cheese on a bagel, it might be best to understand first where cream cheese came from. And for all of you that said 'cows', while that may be funny, ha ha, that's not what I had in mind.

A History of Cream Cheese

Yet another urban legend claims that cream cheese, as we know it today was first created in Chester, New York in the late 1800's. At that time, a form of cream cheese known as Neufchatel was quite popular in France. Neufchatel had been around for centuries– the first official mention of it can be found in the 1543 ledgers of Saint-Aman Abbey of Rouen. Fast forward to 1872. Charles Green, a New York dairyman, wanted to make a better type of the creamy cheese that he could sell in the United States. At that time, there were a few brands already on the market, but Green was on a mission to improve the French version of Neufchatel cheese. He brought a European cheese maker to town, who shared his tips for making better cheese. Another Catskills dairyman, William Lawrence, is said to have eavesdropped on the conversation and jotted down the recipe he was listening to. In his attempt to recreate said recipe, Lawrence accidentally doubled the amount of cream. He liked the result so much that he began selling it under the name "Star Brand Cream Cheese." Over time, the brand name was changed. Though the product was developed in the Catskills, Philadelphia was the most fashionable name in the United States at that time and so Philadelphia Cream Cheese was born

Jeffery Marks writes in his June 10, 2011 article in Food, Culture and Society that: "Cream cheese was not "accidentally invented by William Lawrence in 1872." Directions for making cream cheese can be found in a Pennsylvania newspaper as early as 1769 and in scores of American books, periodicals and cookbooks in the early 1800s. William A. Lawrence was, however, the first to manufacture large quantities of cream cheese due to the technological transformation of the dairy industry during the second half of the 1800s. He first began manufacturing Neufchatel cheese in 1872 and, after being approached by the New York grocery firm, Park & Tilford, to put a richer and more delicate cheese on the market, began by 1875 to make Neufchatel with cream added to it. He called his product "Cream Cheese." Lawrence was aided by a NY distributor, Alvah L. Reynolds, who sold Lawrence's product under the brand name: Philadelphia Cream Cheese. It was not C.D. Reynolds (another NY dairyman) but Alvah Reynolds who bought the Empire Cheese Factory in 1892 in order to go into production for himself. In 1903, Reynolds sold his Philadelphia brand to the Phenix Cheese Co. (who, later, merged with Kraft)."

One thing is for certain, cream cheese, particularly the Philadelphia-brand cheese survives to this day as the most popular American cream cheese on the market, controlling over 70% of the $800 million market. And Kraft, which has been perfecting the cheese for more than 75 years, closely guards its manufacturing secrets, keeping them in a vault in Chicago. What it knows, it isn't sharing.

Types of Schmears

Now this is where the fun begins. There seem to be as many types of schmears as there are people that will eat them. Let's start with the cream cheese schmears.

Another note on cream cheese. In our efforts to get away from fats in our diets, there has been an influx of "lite" cream cheese products. The truth is we need fats in our diets. They are vital to our body function. I am of the opinion, and here is another disclaimer, it is my opinion, that if we ate real fats we would not eat as much other foods. I believe that our hunger increases when our bodies are telling us that we need something, some nutrient or substance that helps our body function. In this case, our body needs fats. I am not a nutritionist and cannot tell you the difference between saturated and unsaturated fats. But

I can say that good fat (whichever that is) satisfies and a person eats less. That does not mean you should go out and eat a pound of cheese and deep fried foods. But giving up fats altogether is clearly not the answer as the amount of obesity in people is on the rise.

Let the letters and emails begin!

Fruit Schmears

Whip up some cream cheese, toss in whatever fruit you like and voila'. The more common fruit schmears are blueberry, strawberry, cranberry and banana. Some bagel cafes also carry more exotic flavors like mango and kiwi and papaya. The types of fruit used appear to be localized. I have not been able to locate a mango schmear in New England, but maybe after reading this book someone can send some.

Savory Schmears

These can get interesting. Before I go any further, I have to admit to a bias for savory schmears and bagels. I love jalapeño and when I can't find a jalapeño bagel, I can often find a jalapeño schmear. There are also a variety of herb schmears with dill, onion and basil that are delicious with lox and onion. Speaking of lox, when none are to be found, there are plenty of salmon schmears that are a good substitute.

Non-Cream Cheese Schmears

Yet another interesting category and why our consumption of bagels has grown by leaps and bounds. Any kind of nut butter is a schmear: peanut, almond are the more familiar and you may want to try one with cashew butter. Tasty.

Other schmears are made with sun-dried tomatoes and feta cheese; there's hummus and tahini for another flavor altogether.

Honestly, can you think of any other food that has this much variety and can satisfy and craving?

5 AND NOW ADD LOX

It was once said that "History is written by the winners," and while I see examples of this (imagine how different our history books would be if the South had won the Civil War) everyone was a winner with regards to lox and how they came to be associated with bagels.

When the Scandinavians brought salmon to the New World, the Jewish community immediately ate it up. Every source I went to online, including the usual suspects (Google, Wikipedia, dictionary.com, Merriam-Webster.com) agree that the salmon was called 'laks' after the Yiddish word for salmon.

There is an interesting article in the Saveur Magazine from 2008 called "Lox Lessons" by Dana Bowen. According to the article: "After the transcontinental railroad started delivering barrels of salted salmon from the Pacific coast to other parts of the country in 1869, the food gained popularity in New York City, particularly among Eastern European Jewish immigrants who had brought with them to this country a love of cured and smoked fish."

Other sources conclude that with the minimal storage and cooking areas available in the tenements where the immigrants lived, any prepared food was like our modern day convenience foods – cheap and easy. The important and most fascinating reason that salmon grew in popularity was that it was 'pareve' meaning it did not break any kosher laws and could be eaten with dairy making it a perfect complement to bagels. All things considered, it is easy to see how lox and bagels became not only a staple, but an important part of the culture and community.

So what exactly is Lox?

Lox is thinly sliced salmon fillet, typically less than 5 millimeters or 0.20 inches and traditionally the belly of Pacific varieties of salmon, usually king, and cured in a very salty brine. The curing with salt traces back to the beginnings of preserving foods when the only way to store and preserve meats was to cure it with salt. Contrary to some reports, real lox is never smoked. Ever. If someone tries to tell you that the smoked salmon is lox, walk away. The best and only lox has the rich salty taste that compliments the bagel, the cream cheese, the tomato, the capers... yummy.

There are traditionalists who think that the only bagels that go with lox are poppy seed or sesame and on rare occasion, plain. In fact, a dear friend will never eat bagels with me again because I dared eat the lox with a pumpernickel bagel and omitted the cream cheese. For all the purists please do continue on with the poppy seed and sesame. At the risk of further reproach from my friends, I will even eat lox with garlic bagels.

It's also interesting to see the growth in popularity in lox.   For one, I cannot think of a single place, especially in New York City, where you can find "cheap" lox. If it is priced lower, it may be smoked or use an inferior piece of salmon. Otherwise, be prepared to open up your wallet when ordering lox.

6 THE PERFECT BAGEL RECIPES

When researching the materials for this book, I found that bagel recipes really did not alter much between one another. The biggest variations were in manner to prepare said bagels. And there were some differing opinions on when to add the toppings and how to do add them. What I have decided then is to list ingredients and how to mix them, then where there are alternatives, offer those as well. Most people, from what I gather, like to experiment with the various methods while they search for their perfect bagel.

And so without further ado... The Perfect Bagel Recipes.

First up: New York Style

Makes 8 bagels

The Essentials:

2 teaspoons of active dry or cake yeast (you can replace with instant yeast, just use 1 ½ teaspoons if you do)

1 ½ tablespoons of sugar (I've seen this as high as 4 tablespoons which is a bit too sweet for me)

1 ¼ cups of warm water (you may need more or less depending on the flour you use and if you live in a higher altitude)

3 ½ cups of bread flour or high gluten flour1 ½ teaspoons of salt

Whisked Egg for adding toppings (optional)

The Optional Toppings:

Caraway, poppy or sesame seeds, salt (I like coarse sea salt), chopped or minced fresh garlic or onion.

The Steps to Getting There:

1. In ½ cup of the warm water, pour in the sugar and yeast but do not stir. Let it sit for five to ten minutes or until you see a frothy foam. Once that happens, stir the mixture, until the sugar and yeast are dissolved in the water.

2. Combine the flour and salt in a large bowl. Make a well in the middle and pour in the yeast and sugar mixture.

3. Pour half of the remaining warm water into the well. Now start to mix in the flour to the water taking a little flour from each side and stirring it in. Add the remaining water as needed. Depending on where you live (higher altitudes for example) you may need more water; add just a little at a time. The end result you are looking for is a moist

(not sticky) yet firm dough.

4. On a floured countertop, knead the dough for about 10 minutes until it is smooth and elastic. Try working in as much flour as possible to form a firm and stiff dough. There should not be any sign of the 'moist' we were going for in step three.

5. Coat a large bowl with oil and turn the dough inside the bowl to coat. Cover the bowl with a damp dish cloth. Let the dough rise in a warm place for 1 hour, until the dough has doubled in size. Punch the dough down, and let it rest for another 10 minutes.

6. Divide the dough into 8 pieces. If you want to be precise, use a scale or if not, you can 'eyeball' to go for consistency. Shape each piece into a round. The goal is to get a round ball. You can roll it in your hands or on the surface where you are working. Do this with each of the pieces.

7. Using your finger or a knife or some other tool gently press into the center of each dough ball to form a ring. Stretch the ring to about 1/4 to 1/3 the diameter of the bagel and place on a lightly oiled cookie sheet. Do this with each of the pieces.

8. After shaping the dough rounds and placing them on the cookie sheet, cover with a damp kitchen towel and allow to rest for an additional 10 minutes. Meanwhile, bring a large pot of water to boil and preheat your oven to 425ºF / 220ºC / Gas Mark 7.

9. After the water comes to a vigorous rolling boil, reduce the heat. Use a large slotted spoon to lower the bagels into the water, one at a time. Depending on the size of the pot you are using, add as many that will allow you to turn and maneuver the bagels around without crushing them. Once the bagels are in, it should only take a few seconds for them

to float to the top. Let them sit there for 1 minute, and then flip them over to boil for another minute. If you like really chewy bagels extend the boiling times to 2 minutes each side. Variation note: Some people add sugar, honey or malt to the boiling water. This is a carryover from the original bagel recipes that changed during the shortages of World War I. Some bakers went back to that method after the war, but bagels that are known as New York-Style do not add sugar to the water. Montreal Bagels do include some type of sugar in the boiling water.

10. As you take the bagel from the boiling water, place them on a lightly oiled baking sheet.

11. Now for the fun stuff. If you want to top your bagels with any optional ingredient, the time is now, before they are placed in the oven. Take your whisked egg and brush the bagels to be topped with a slight coating of egg. For plain bagels, you can pass on the egg. Unless of course you want to try the egg wash. Then, take the topping of your choice and sprinkle on the egg brushed boiled dough.

12. Bake for 20 minutes, until golden brown. Notice the wonderful aroma filling your kitchen and home... my mouth is starting to water...

13. Place fresh baked bagels on a wire rack to cool. Try to wait until they are at least cool to touch. Then enjoy!
I'm hungry already.

Variations

With the introduction of blueberry, cranberry, pesto, cinnamon raisin and other ingredients, the recipe will change. You may need to cut down on sugar if using fruit or increase the sugar (as with the case of sugar cinnamon bagels).

Gluten-Free

Some people have asked me about using gluten-free flour in bagel recipes. While I am a fan of gluten-free products and have found some delicious recipes for baked goods, I still cannot fathom a gluten-free bagel. Bagels are meant to be gluten rich (as shown by the need for high-gluten bread flours). Protein rich gluten is what combines to make that wonderful yeast and dough aroma that only freshly baking bread brings. It reminds me of the cold winter mornings in New York and Connecticut with frost on the windows, a fire burning in the fireplace and hot coffee in my mug. The warm oven and baking bread fills the entire house with mouthwatering gluten filled bread. Rice, potato to rye floured breads just does not have the same effect.

As I said earlier – experiment. I'd also recommend cutting the recipe in half for the times you are testing different mixtures. If you do have some suggestions that work, including a combination of gluten-free flours that work, email me at bagelladdy@thepsychologyofbagels.com and I'll update the book and add them to the web site.

Next Up: Montreal Bagels

Makes 18 bagels

The Essentials:

1 ½ cups water at room temperature

2 packages dry quick-rising yeast (or 1 ½ ounces fresh yeast)

1 teaspoon sugar

2 ½ teaspoons salt

1 whole egg

1 egg yolk

¼ cup oil

½ cup honey

5 cups or more flour (preferably bread flour)

1/3 cup honey or malt syrup

Sesame or poppy seeds for sprinkling on top

The Steps to Getting There:

1. In a large mixing bowl blend together the water, yeast, sugar and salt. Stir in the whole egg, the yolk, oil and ½ cup honey, and mix well.

2. Add the 5 cups flour, and mix until the dough until it is soft and moist, but not sticky. Transfer to a lightly floured work surface and knead to form a firm, stiff dough.

3. When the dough is smooth and elastic, place it in a lightly oiled bowl, and cover with a damp kitchen towel.

4. Let the dough rest about 20 minutes. Punch it down, and divide into 18 equal portions.

5. Fill a large pot with water and add the remaining 1/3 cup of honey or malt syrup. Heat the water to a vigorous rolling boil. Then cover and reduce the heat allowing the water to simmer while preparing the bagels.

6. Shape the dough portions into bagels or doughnut-like rings by rolling each portion into an 8- to 10-inch long strip that is 3/4 inch thick. Fold or coil the ends over each other and press with the palm of one hand and rolling back and forth gently to seal. This step locks the ends together and must be done properly or the bagels will open while being

boiled. Once formed, let the bagels rest another 15 minutes on a towel-lined baking sheet.

7. Preheat oven to 450°. Bring the water back to a boil and remove the lid. Have bowls of poppy seeds and sesame seeds nearby.

8. When the water is boiling vigorously, use a slotted spoon and add the bagels to the water. Add only as many as will fit so that you can turn them without crushing. As they rise to the surface, turn them over, and let them boil an additional minute before removing them and quickly dipping them in either bowl of the seeds. Continue boiling the bagels until all have been boiled and seeded. If you don't want any seeds, just place them on the baking sheet after you take them out of the water. Note: You do not need to brush Montreal bagels with an egg wash after boiling. The sugar in the water provides the 'glue' that holds the seeds to the dough.

9. Arrange the boiled bagels on a baking sheet, and bake on the lowest rack of oven until they are medium brown, approximately 25 minutes. Enjoy the slightly sweet scent as aroma of baking bagels fills your home.

10. Remove the golden, crusty treats from the oven. Place bagels on a wire rack to cool and try to wait before biting into one. They are delicious!

7

BAGELS IN OUR LIVES:
A LOVE STORY

While doing the research for this book, I met several people with fascinating stories about something that happened in their life that centered on bagels. I had no idea that bagels really meant a great deal to so many people. At that point, bagels were one of my favorite breakfast foods and most people I know seemed to enjoy them. But to hear so many stories that people actually took the time to remember? Who knew?

It seemed that further research was needed to understand this phenomenon.

It's clear that food is an important part of our lives. Beyond the obvious that we need food and the nutrients it provides in order to survive, food has become a defining source for most people. We are known by the cuisine we enjoy or not. And for most people in our culture, we have food in abundance and so we use food to define and shape us. Sometimes literally. Food carries labels – whether it be based on ethnicity or composition, it is categorized and it is these same categories that can define our community, certainly our tastes and definitely our experiences.

Is there anyone on this planet that does not think of bagels as being a Jewish food? Culturally, bagels have a great history in the Jewish community although its origins in Poland do not go so far as to define which particular groups created or feasted on the beloved beygls. Some sources say that it was only the Jewish communities, others aren't that specific. The one thing that is certain is that it was Jewish immigrants that brought the beygls to North America and built a following for them once here. That's not to say that other religious groups and ethnicities did not enjoy them; rather that the Jewish community is the most associated with them. It was also the Jewish community that added the ever so thinly sliced smoked salmon, a favorite of fellow Scandinavian immigrants, to the beygls thus starting a tradition that has not only lasted all these many years, it has thrived and grown. In fact, lox is a derivation the Yiddish word 'laks' which means 'salmon'. Can you imagine it being anything else but the beloved lox and bagels with cream cheese, capers and tomato and, for those reckless enough, thinly sliced cucumbers or onion? I know I can't. What's fascinating is that bagels have transcended the Jewish culture to where just about everyone has tried or even loves bagels and makes them a part of their weekly meals. Regardless of your ethnic background or religious leaning, who hasn't enjoyed a warm bagel with cream cheese?

With the advent of the many bagels specialty shops, anybody can stop by and get a baker's dozen, a couple of schmears and be on their way for a weekend brunch or a family gathering. Weekday's finds line of people waiting at

Einstein's, Murray's, Noah's or Zaro's for a hot cuppa something and a lightly toasted plain/sesame/poppy seed bagel with cream cheese. Plain cream cheese of course and never ever fat free.

So it wasn't surprising when people started telling me some of their favorite bagel stories. Here are a few actual stories that have only been edited for grammar and punctuation. If you want to send me your favorite bagel story, do so at keepitfresh@thepsychologyofbagels.com.

A Baby and His Bagel

"When I was an infant, I would not drink milk or nurse. My mother tried everything and as you can imagine, I was not gaining the weight a baby ought to gain. Plus, I cried a lot, maybe because I was hungry! In a panic, she, my mother, told me how she wrapped me up in warm blankets to take to me to the doctor. I was the middle of January in Seattle and I imagine it being pretty cold. Anyway, she takes me to the doctor who does an exam and after he pokes and prods, tells her to give me a bagel.

"Bagel?" When she tells the story I hear how incredulous she sounds and wonder how a young new mother must sound when her doctor tells her something so strange.

"Yes, bagel." He repeats and in the retelling, I wonder if she thinks he called her an idiot for questioning him. "Get as freshly baked as you can or make them yourself. Take the dough out of the center and make a mash of it with warm milk and a touch of fresh butter. Then feed that to him. It will not only give him some much needed nutrition, it should spark his ability to eat by working his facial muscles. It should even stop some of the crying which I suspect is his way of telling you he's hungry. Other than that, I can't see anything wrong with him. And don't worry; sometimes it takes a newborn a few days, even a couple of weeks to figure out this eating thing. A bagel, with the yeast and flour should trigger a response."

My mother bundled me up again and on our way from the doctor to our home, she stopped at a bagel shop and asked for the freshest bagels they had. Apparently, they had just taken poppy seed out of the oven and they were cooling for a few minutes before they added them to the others. My mother asked for three and took them home. Once there, she settled me in my basket while she warmed the milk and prepared the mash.

It worked. Mom sounded so very surprised in the retelling, but it seemed I enjoyed the mixture so much, she called the bagel shop and asked for another dozen to be sent. I have always wondered one thing....

Is that why even today my favorite bagel is toasted poppy seed with butter?"

Greg, Seattle Washington

Here's my view of the history of the bagel:
God said to the Jews: "You WILL suffer....but...I will give you the bagel"
As to my favorite bagel(s), as a person who grew up on the lower east side of New York, I cannot abide anything but the traditional flavors I grew up with...forget blueberry or cinnamon, or any of the stuff with pesto or cheese. I love pumpernickel, onion or garlic. Period. Even though it is my favorite, I generally forgo garlic because it is quite strong on the breath. The last time I indulged in a garlic bagel, it was right before my first appointment. I went to East Coast Bagel in the Marina and got one toasted with cream cheese. It was almost gone by the time I made it

home and boy was it delicious. The cream cheese blended perfectly with the garlic and these guys know how to make a garlic bagel. Lots of real crushed garlic baked right on top. Anyway, I walked into my office, took out my toothbrush and ran to restroom to brush my teeth before my appointment arrived. Didn't work. My client came in and immediately wrinkled her nose. I've long thought that garlic lovers have no idea how strong the smell is; we are somehow immune to what really smells awful to others. That was it for me. I gave up garlic bagels and now it's a true toss-up between pumpernickel and onion...depends on my mood.

Amy, Venice California

Maintaining Composure in Cleveland

A one day business trip to Cleveland starting with a 6:30 a.m. departure is a challenge for this non-morning person in and of itself. I accomplished getting to the airport on time and well before any food establishments were open, only to find the plane delayed. The delay was long enough that the restaurants opened and I had time for a quick (hopefully eye opening) breakfast. When the shops opened I decided to comfort myself with a bagel --- poppy seed with butter. I stood at a counter, half asleep, managing my purse, briefcase and bagel and...dropped the bagel. My reflexes (and love of bagels) took over ... causing me to grab and pull the bagel (butter side up) into my chest.

And there I was in a linen dress, with a perfect bagel imprint across my chest and no time to take a taxi home to change. I did manage a trip to the bathroom for repairs ... resulting in a perfect bagel imprint with little flecks of paper towel now imbedded in the linen. I laughed at the image thinking it looked more like a sesame seed bagel rather than the poppy seed I had chosen. Oh well, I ate my bagel, enjoying it immensely, wondering how I was going to explain the unwanted stain on my clothing.

Upon arrival in our Cleveland offices, I spent the first five minutes of introductions going for the "school girl" look -- holding a folder cross-armed over the offending area. I quickly concluded this was not a posture I could maintain all day long and that I needed to think about the substance of the meeting and not my bagel. So ... I said to my hosts "I have a funny story to tell you" and proudly displayed my bagel badge of courage. This broke the ice and promptly and permanently removed any potential intimidation factor related to the arrival of someone from DC Headquarters. But there were unforeseen and sad consequences; I haven't eaten a bagel in an airport since.

Carol, Washington DC

Are you a victim of BRI?

That would be Bagel Related Injury – an absolutely honest-to-God-I-cannot-make-this-stuff-up – ailment. It's even tracked at emergency rooms around the country. And believe it or not, the highest rate of occurrences falls on Sunday. I found this in my online searches:

"The number one injury in the Long Island emergency rooms on Sunday mornings was knife wounds from improperly cutting a bagel." Posted at "Beware brunch" Richard Goldfarb, Food Liability Law Blog.

Other posts on the site claim that BRI has more reported incidents than burns from the coffee at McDonalds with one person saying when he was being treated for the coffee burns, the doctor commented on how nicely the scar from his bagel accident was healing. So what does that tell you?

And from Freakonomics:

"Americans ate an estimated 3 billion bagels at home in 2011, an average of about 11 per person (this doesn't include bagels eaten at work). And in the course of slicing up all those bagels, almost 2,000 people cut their fingers so badly that they ended up in an emergency room. By the finger-cut-to-E.R. metric, that makes bagel-cutting the fifth most dangerous activity in the American kitchen. So it shouldn't be surprising that an array of home gadgets have arrived on the scene to prevent bagel-related injuries."

One bit of advice... make sure you are fully AWAKE before grabbing a knife to cut your bagel. Please.

Friars Club Beverly Hills

My favorite bagel experience is sadly no more. My dad would take me to the old Friars Club in Beverly Hills. There wasn't a place like it; old Hollywood started the place and with the changing times, lost the place. But that's another story for another time. You asked me about bagels. In the late 90's the Friars Club on Charleville and Little Santa Monica had many events and if you were a member or a guest, you could go there any time during the day. They had a never ending supply of coffee and bagels. And their bagels were unique. Not in flavor. No these guys were traditionalists. Only New York style and only four types: plain, sesame, poppy seed or pumpernickel. There was a tray of them, already sliced and what I liked to call "gutted" meaning, they had removed the inner dough leaving just enough of the bread and mostly the crust. I'd pop it in the toaster, just for a minute or two to warm it up, then fill it will cream cheese and capers, add tomato and some of the best lox in the world. Absolutely delicious. It was such a shame when they closed the place. I never found out where they got the bagels and lox, but I can certainly gut the bagel wherever I am. I wonder to this day why other places don't serve them that way.

Karen, Los Angeles

Oh! Canada

I may be among the few, especially here in California, but the only bagels for me are from Montreal. I like the texture and crunch. For some reason, the puffy New York style bagels feel much heavier to me. But hey that's my taste. As for my favorite experience, my wife is from England. Bagels there are a rarity and from what she tells me, don't compare to any style we have here. The rub is that she loves New York-style and often picks some up from Izzy's Bagels in Fountain Valley. She knows I am not a fan and will bring me a bialy or health bar which is more to my taste, yet really is a poor substitute to my favorite black seed bagels.

When she left for Izzy's. I was busy making coffee and setting out plates and knives when I heard the garage door open. She walked in carrying a box and a small bag that I knew was from the bagel shop.

"Here," she said placing the small box in front of me.

I noticed the label. It was from St-Viateur Bagels in Montreal. I smiled at her. "What's this?"

"Just open it."

I did and found in special packaging, one dozen of my favorite black seed bagels. The look on my face must have been one of wonder and awe because she just laughed while she grabbed her coffee mug and poured. When I still could only look at her in great love and gratitude, she said, "Now maybe you can enjoy our Saturday ritual. At least for a couple of weeks. We can order more when you run low."

She continued that smile all through breakfast while I slower savored my favorite bagel.

Larry, Fountain Valley, CA.

An Homage to Bagels

In doing research for this book and web site, I entered the words: "bagel statistics" in the Google toolbar. I found a blog called "Bagel Belly Blog" and was excited to click the link with the hope that someone that loved bagels was actually studying them. The truth was even better... The tag line of the blog is: One man and his bagel. And the blog teaches you how to get statistics from your own blog using some interesting data coding techniques. The picture I now have in my mind is of someone sitting at their computer with beverage and bagel in hand, typing away. Now that's a bagel lover.

The Triple Bagel

What does bagels have to do with tennis? Do players eat three bagels to "carb up" before a big match? Has someone discovered that eating three bagels gives you a competitive edge? Is there a superstition around bagels? All of these questions came to mind when in my research I found that there is, in tennis, what is known as a "Triple Bagel." Excited, I clicked on the link: www.tennis.ukf.net and found this explanation:

"A triple bagel is a match in which the winner(s) wins three complete sets 6-0, 6-0, 6-0 without losing a game (otherwise known as a "whitewash"). The loser's games score looks like a bagel. According to Bud Collins' Tennis Encyclopedia, the term bagel was first used by Eddie Dibbs in the 1970s. The triple bagel is rare nowadays. This is because even the worst player out of the 128 entrants in the draw is usually good enough to at least hold his serve a couple of times in a match against a top seed. There have been no triple bagels in Grand Slam events since 1993. In the open era there have only been five, three of them occurring in 1987. However, back in the early 20th century triple bagels were commonplace."

"Lox and Bagels – The Breakfast of Time Travelers"

No book about bagels would be complete without a shout out to bagels in the media. And in the middle of writing this book one of my favorite nerd sitcoms of all time provided me with the best example. The Big Bang Theory is one of those shows that captures all the clichés of our culture and beats them to a pulp. In the process, I laugh, sometimes uproariously, at the modern-day nerd making their way in our techno-geek world. It's brilliant and funny and so unapologetically over the top and provided me with the best example of this section of the book.

In this particular episode that I saw in reruns because, yes, I like the show so much I even watch the reruns – when I tell you I saw this particular rerun while visiting England I will do so giving you full permission to judge and otherwise make fun of my guilty pleasure – our heroes – Leonard, Sheldon, Howard and Raj – just purchased a life-sized version of the time machine seen in the classic movie, The Time Machine. In their enthusiasm to 'play' with their life size toy, Raj and Howard show up at Leonard's and Sheldon's apartment where said machine resided carrying bags, obviously of food. Howard (last name Wolowitz) exclaims, "I brought lox and bagels, the breakfast of time travelers!"

That one line told you everything about our characters, their history and their personalities. It was perfect, and so deliciously captured the charm of our nerds. And even though it was not clearly stated, I'd bet money it was a Sunday morning.

8 WHAT EXACTLY IS THE PSYCHOLOGY OF BAGELS?

And now we reach the real motivation for writing *The Psychology of Bagels*. When I started on this journey it was with the utmost curiosity and desire to understand how people related to their bagels. Ever since that fateful day at the office when the majority of our group preferred cinnamon raisin bagels, I had to know why. It struck a chord that a number of people with similar backgrounds liked the same food. I wondered if our food interests were based on ethnicity, culture, religion, dysfunctional families, and peer pressure or if we simply like what we like. Greg from Seattle enjoys poppy seed bagels to this day. Is it because they somehow remind him in the deep part of his brain of his mother's concern when he was an infant? Does Larry like Montreal bagels because of some unspoken issue with pillowy bread? Were the people on our team at the office simply avoiding standing out? I wondered if they were to be found at a bagel shop over the weekend would they still eat cinnamon raisin bagels.

Still, I suspect that there are underlying reasons as to why I am a sundried tomato bagel and others prefer plain. Some people steeped in tradition refuse to eat anything but sesame, poppy seed or plain bagels. Anything else is blasphemous. As I dug deeper into the root cause, I found that I need much more information. How else was I going to make what amounts to an educated guess?

Armed with this new found curiosity, I embarked on this journey of discovery and now ask you:

What is your favorite bagel?

It is an important question and one that requires thought and reflection.

Consider the phrase: "You are what you eat." That phrase applies to bagel consumption in such a unique and elegant way.

Take a moment and think about it. There are several types and varieties of bagels. Not only that, bagels have an unmatched ability to alter their appearance whether through expanding the number of varieties or adapting to the ever changing food and taste demands of the people that devour them. New flavors of bagels are added all the time with some highly creative and innovative bagel bakers encouraging their patrons to request new flavors that aren't on their current menu. The sky is the limit with the numerous combinations of food that can make their way to the bagel community. How long before we see a bacon bits bagel, peanut butter, pistachio or even something with mint? Don't laugh – it could happen and I bet you a lifetime supply of bagels that someone in the world tried to make one or more of these flavors. [1]

Food preferences often follow many social, ethical and

historic pathways. Do you prefer sweet or savory? Are you someone that wants cinnamon sugar with sugar sprinkled on top that you can just bite into the pillowy softness without any toasting or schmearing? Does your mouth water thinking about an everything bagel toasted with cream cheese melting over the edges? Are you more of a traditionalist that only eats sesame, poppy seed or plain? Or are you a yuppie seeking the perfect pesto bagel with just a touch of lite cream cheese? Do you like the plump, pillowy texture of the classic New York Style or are you forever thinking about a black seed Montreal bagel?

There are people who are all consumed with having either a savory or a sweet bagel. I for one do not enjoy bagels with any kind of sugar, preferring instead the sumptuousness of a sun-dried tomato or garlic or even a bagel that has it all. Do my particular consumption tastes say anything about me? Bet on it.

Adding another dimension to the discussion: bagels are not only a complete food, they are now accepted as a certified stand-alone meal having transcended breakfast toast status. What other food can make that claim? Chances are you like the same bagels as people that have similar backgrounds and experiences.

Asked another way: Are you a bagel dog or a tuna on toasted rye bagel?

Let's face it. Any of you reading this has a favorite bagel that you prefer. You know the one; it catches your eye the minute you walk into a bagel shop. When you are standing in line at Starbucks, Coffee Bean or Caribou or anywhere else and you see your favorite in the food case, admit it – you'd be tempted to buy it toasted with cream cheese or butter (or just bite into it for the freaks out there) to go with your latte fix. It's the bagel that when you get to the office on bagel day you rifle through the bag seeking your perfect flavor and heave a sigh of relief when you find it –

or cuss under your breath if it's not there.

If you're one of the urban professionals with a palate for the gourmet bagels (sun-dried tomato, pesto of the savory spectrum; pumpkin, apple raisin or cinnamon sugar for the sweet toothed among you) chances are you have a backup flavor that you can actually resist. But when you spy that Asiago or chocolate chip in the case you have no choice. The taste buds engage and automatic pilot clicks on and you are hooked. That bagel is yours so you buy it and savor every delicious bite as it rolls over your tongue and into your stomach. Satisfied. Fulfilled. Happy.

Unless you are a hard core traditionalist whose choices include only sesame, plain or poppy seed[2] most people patronize their favorite bagel shop based on said bagel shop carrying their favorite flavor. That includes schmears, too. If you like a jalapeno schmear and the bagel shop five miles out of your way have it, that's where you stop.

Some can even resist the standard bagels if their favorite flavor is not included in the mix. For those of you with this great capacity to resist the unique bagel aroma, especially when smothered in perfectly whipped cream cheese, I say relax and get over yourself. Eating is one of life's greatest pleasures. Eating bagels is a joy.

For the diet conscious you can easily enjoy your bagel and eat sensibly the rest of the day; or take another fifteen minutes on the tread mill at the gym. Either way, denying yourself this simple delicious treasure just shows how rigid and uptight you are.

C'mon. Have fun and eat a bagel.

And in the meantime, take the quiz that you will find at www.thepsychologyofbagels.com and at the end of the book to see where you fit with all the other bagel lovers around the world.

Based on your responses, I will publish my findings in *The Psychology of Bagels: The Results.*

[1]Yes, I admit to trying to make a bacon bits bagel. It wasn't half bad actually...

[2]Okay, I'll throw in cinnamon raisin here simply because they are so popular. But for the record, a true hard core traditionalist would scoff at the notion.

9 WHAT IS YOUR BAGEL?

We know you struggle with this question, and we are here to help you sort that out. We've developed a quiz using all the most highly scientific analytical capabilities known to man, with questions so distinctly considered and written that it promises to be accurate to within plus or minus 100 points. In other words, it's all in fun and simply compares you to every other bagel fan in the world (or at least all those that have taken the quiz...) and shows you how you match up with them. When you take our quiz, you'll find the answer to that very question: What is your favorite bagel?

You will find a copy of the quiz in the appendix but I highly encourage you to go to www.thepsychologyofbagels.com and complete the quiz online.

And if the answer we give you is not even in the same savory vs. sweet category then you can take pride in being the maverick, the loner, that Renaissance person that forges your own pathway in life and in eating.

Or you can say that this is all just scientific hooey. Regardless of your feelings, all results will be published in *The Psychology of Bagels: The Results.* So send in many responses as often as you like. The goal is to once and for all know why we eat the bagels we eat.

10 THE ONE AND ONLY BAGEL QUIZ

Take the following quiz to determine your bagel type.

1. What is your occupation?

   a. Student

   b. Consultant

   c. Managerial

   d. Administrative

   e. Teacher

   f. Doctor/Nurse/Medical

   g. Construction

   h. Does getting out of bed every day count as a job?

   i. Other

2. What time of day are you most alert?

   a. I love to watch the sun rise!

   b. Don't talk to me until 10:00am at the earliest.

   c. I don't get cranking until 4 o'clock

   d. Who who! Night Owl

3. What is your attitude towards religion?

a. Agnostic

b. Atheist

c. Practice regularly

d. Non-practicing religious/spiritual

e. Other

4. Where do you currently live? (State)

5. What is your favorite morning beverage?

a. Coffee - black

b. Coffee – white (Google it if you don't know what it means)

c. Espresso drink

d. I add so much cream and sugar to regular coffee I might as well get a Latte

e. Tea

f. Milk

g. Juice

h. Other

6. When are you most likely to enjoy a bagel?

a. Breakfast

b. Lunch – perfect sandwich

c. Bagel dog

d. Bagel Pizza

e. I eat them all the time!

f. Other

7. What is your relationship status?

a. Married

b. Single

c. Divorced

d. Widowed

e. Actively involved with someone

f. Available and looking – want my photo?

g. Other

8. What do you like to read?

a. Fiction

b. Non-fiction

c. News/magazines

d. Blogs

e. Do cereal boxes count?

9. What kind of pet do you own?

a. Cat

b. Dog

c. Bird

d. Fish

e. Reptiles

f. Sharks

g. Dinosaurs that I cloned

h. Other

10. What's your preferred method of communicating with friends and family? (Check all that apply)

a. Text

b. Email

c. Snail mail

d. Phone

e. Fax

f. Facebook

g. Skype

h. Twitter

i. Telepathically

11. I'm on: (check all that apply)

a. Facebook

b. My Space

c. LinkedIn

d. You Tube

e. Google

f. Blogger

g. Skype

h. Flickr

i. Twitter

j. Shutterbug

k. Digg

l. Redditt

m. Wikis

12. What type of cell phone or tablet do you have? (Check all that apply)

a. Basic

b. Smartphone

c. IPhone

d. Android

e. IPad

f. Why do I need any of these? I have a land line...

13. How many apps do you have?

a. 1-10

b. 11-25

c. 26-50

d. 51+

e. I refuse to get any apps. So there.

14. What types of apps do you own (check all that apply)

a. Games & Entertainment

b. Music

c. Food related

d. Money Money Money

e. Travel/GPS/Maps

f. Shopping

g. Weather

h. Fitness and Health

i. Sports and Recreational

j. Business Apps

k. Other

15. What eReader do you own?

a. Kindle

b. Nook

c. iPad

d. Sony

e. Xoom

f. Galaxy Tab

g. Again with the reading...

16. Are you a Mac or PC user?

    a. Mac

    b. PC

    c. I'm really too old for this

17. Do you regularly access any of the following? (Check all that apply)

    a. Twitter account

    b. My own website

    c. You Tube

    d. My blog

    e. A friend's blog

    f. Nope Nada Nothing – now leave me alone, will you?

Favorite Bagel Quiz Part 2					
How often do you:	**Never**	**Sometimes**	**Neutral**	**Often**	**Always**
Play team sports with people from work and/or school (softball, football, etc. Drinking games aren't included)					
Work up a sweat (must involve some physical activity)					
Go to Happy Hour at your favorite watering hole					
Travel outside your community					
Travel outside your city or state					
Travel to a foreign country					

How often do you:	Never	Sometimes	Neutral	Often	Always
Travel outside the building you live in					
Go on weekend getaways					
Watch sitcoms					
Watch reality television					
Watch DWTS					
Watch American Idol					
Care who got the final rose on the Bachelor or Bachelorette					
Go to the movies					
Play games on your computer or phone					
Text your family					
Text your friends					
Text your boss					

How often do you:	Never	Sometimes	Neutral	Often	Always
Call in sick from work					
Work more than 40 hours per week at your job					
Commute daily to your place of work					
Use public transportation to get to work					
Use public transportation for running errands or other activities					
Surf the Internet at work					
Shop online while at work					
Update Facebook while at work					
Tweet while at work					

How often do you:	Never	Sometimes	Neutral	Often	Always
Skip breakfast					
Go to your favorite coffee place					
Have juice in the morning					
Eat the same type of bagel all the time. Variety is over rated.					
Eat cream cheese on your bagel.					
Toast your bagel					
Have a bagel at lunch					
Enjoy bagel dogs (counts double if you know what a bagel dog is)					
Buy bagels for the people in your office					

How often do you:	Never	Sometimes	Neutral	Often	Always
Go out of your way for a genuine New York-style bagel even though there is a bagel shop on the corner					
Know what a Montreal-style bagel is					
Eat Montreal-style bagels					
Have a bagel for breakfast					
Buy packaged bagels at the supermarket					
Use "lite" cream cheese					
Use fruit-flavored cream cheese (i. e. blueberry or strawberry)					
Use jalapeno cream cheese					

How often do you:	Never	Sometimes	Neutral	Often	Always
Use the word 'schmear' instead of cream cheese					
I only eat breakfast when someone brings bagels to the office					
Eat spinach pesto or sundried tomato bagels					
Make your own bagels					
Eat bagels on the weekend					
Think about bagels at home at night while watching television					
Only eat New York-style bagels					
Eat chocolate chip bagels					

How often do you:	Never	Sometimes	Neutral	Often	Always
Think quizzes like this are really stupid but I play along anyway					
Get a free bagel for taking a quiz like this...					

ABOUT THE AUTHOR

Writer and self-proclaimed bagel lover, Carrie KC West first knew she had to understand how this wondrous food fit into our world while observing strange behaviors of people consuming said treat. Inspiration grew to an all-consuming drive to understand this simple yet interesting meal.